LET GO
OF YOUR BAGGAGE
AND
TRAVEL LIGHT

A Manual for Changing Your Life

CECILE MCLAUGHLIN
and
VICTOR MULL

TRAVEL LIGHT PRESS
DENVER, COLORADO

Published by Travel Light Press
5740 East 6th Avenue
Denver, Colorado 80220

Book Design and Production by
Canyon Graphics, Box 8878, Aspen, Colorado 81612

Library of Congress Catalog Card Number: 91-65410

Printed in the United States of America

First printing: April, 1991

ISBN 1-879838-00-1

91 92 93 94 95 / 10 9 8 7 6 5 4 3 2 1

I do acknowledge
all my teachers and guides,
both Earthly and Heavenly,
who have given so much;
without them this book
would not have materialized.

Cecile McLaughlin
April, 1991

*This book is dedicated
to my dear and loving family
who have given me
much love and support
when I was truly in need.*

Prayer

Dear loving ones, Mother Father God, teachers and guides:

It is my desire this day that I may know who I am, that I may know and be that divine entity, one with Source who is in the service of the Lord most high at all times.

I ask that I may open my heart and mind to that guidance that is there for me at all times, that I may know those ways in which I may best serve. I ask that I may know that the way of service need not be difficult, unless in blindness, I do choose to see those ways as difficult. That I may know the choice is always mine. I may just as easily experience service in joy and exaltation.

I ask that this day I may be aware of that higher energy that is available to me and does surround me. That I may know this powerful energy of love does attract to me each moment of the day that which is most beneficial to me.

Let my heart be open to receive that which is given to me. That I give openly, joyously, and in full measure in return.

I ask these dear ones that I may release those fears of relating in an open loving way at all times.

That I may remember that much has been given to me and I may give in return. For truly it is a joy to give and a joy to receive. And one is not healing without the other, nor does one grow in divine spirit one without the other.

When the flow is stopped in either direction that divine energy is damned up and becomes more dense and eventually can cause pain, physical illness, and deterioration. For all things that are in a proper state of health are constantly growing and changing. It is only when things get out of balance that the machinery wears out.

Love is the great mender. To give and receive in love does bring things back into balance. The way each entity feels about himself is projected out into the world. If one has love for self, love will be projected out into the world and will attract those entities to him who also have self love. If one has self hate, self hate will be projected out and will attract those entities who have self hate.

If you find yourself in an abusive situation you must ask yourself why you are attracting this to self. The answer may be in past programming of family, friends, loves, teachers, figures of authority in church or state. Some may come from many lives past, and may reflect guilt from past times when one did not live up to what his inner knowing told him was the appropriate behavior.

Mass consciousness has much programming to the affect that the individual who does not follow those figures in authority to the letter, be it teacher, parent, head of state or church are guilty of imperfections and therefore unworthy of love or complete acceptance.

There are many levels of self approval ranging from a little self approval now and then to a lot of self approval and finally to one who is enlightened or very close to enlightenment. Those who are enlightened, or close to enlightenment, love themselves and their fellow man with an openness that demands nothing in return. This entity no longer depends on outside information to tell him he is good or bad, worthy or unworthy. He does not need that feedback from those about him. For he knows he is a divine entity of light and knows those judgements from outside do not affect him one way or another.

From this comes his power. He is freed of many limitations. He can make his own choices without fear of condemnation, he can make his own choices without the need to please those about him. Approval or disapproval does not touch him. He is free to honor himself and free of those needs to manipulate, control, coerce, or subjugate those about him. He is an open loving entity and can make those decisions he needs to make from a center of love and not need.

There are times when one is on the road to enlightenment and struggling to come from self loathing to self approval that there is a need for outside props to help one to feel he has others' approval. Physical proofs like driving a certain type of car, attending a prestigious school, wearing the "right" clothing. Those are things that many equate as symbols of a worthy successful entity and for a time they may be necessary for an entity struggling for self approval. It is appropriate if he feels the need of these things to give them to self. To deprive self of those things when they could be available only says, "you can't have these things because you are unworthy, or perhaps deny yourself because of guilt that you may have more than your neighbor."

What does happen, as one approaches enlightenment, is that the need for these props drops away as they become aware of their true being and worth. At that point they are freed of self imposed limitations, they can choose or not choose to possess the physical objects that mankind does often surround himself. However, there is no virtue in poverty or deprivation. If one feels virtue in self deprecation he is deluding himself and feeling self righteous in the delusion. Some entities may choose to travel through life very lightly because of the ease and freedom they feel, not being burdened with a lot of physical goods. Both attitudes are equally appropriate when a choice is made from within not to prove how worthy they have become, are becoming, or would like to be.

Eventually each entity on the path to enlightenment will come to know that worthiness is not something that one can achieve. Worthiness is that state in which man came forth. It was only as man felt himself separated from God that unworthiness manifested in the thoughts and feelings of man. It has been encouraged by many of mankind who desire power. Many in powerful positions in the state and church play upon those feelings of unworthiness to gain and keep positions of power. In this way the masses are kept in bondage and through fear accept and cooperate with those in power to give up their own personal power and to abdicate personal responsibility for themselves.

Limitations, Worthiness

Know from the center of your being that you are worthy of all things, that you are one with Divine Source, that nothing, nothing is withheld from you in any way. Know that you are truly one, one with all that is, you are a part of us and all that we have is yours. You are divine, with all of the love, light and power of a divine being.

The veil of unworthiness that you put on and wear like sack cloth and ashes does not represent what or who you are. You were created to wear a shining garment of white, to walk upon the earth without bruising your feet, to have flowers spring up in your footsteps, the animals and birds to eat from your hand. This is who you truly are, accept this vision of yourself and make it your own.

You have been on a long path for eons and eons of time. But now you are coming home! Home! Be filled with joy for this is home to the Father, who has waited long for your return. Man has wandered in the desert with only rare impressions of what his true heritage might be and now it is time to come home, home to your rightful position as the Father's Co-creator. Home to your heritage and you are nearly there, just a few more doors to open and the veil will be lifted. Even now you see through dimly and know that we are waiting with arms outstretched, to hold you and to welcome you home. You are one of our own.

We would have you think upon these things: All which you ask for is already given. All that we have is yours also. We tell you there are no limitations upon which you may receive. Those limitations which you perceive are not limitations put forth by us, your loving friends and guides. They are limitations that you, upon the planet earth, called into being and have not yet released.

So it is with all mankind. On the dark path which he has trod, not knowing that he may call upon the light. His fears and his lack of self worth and self appreciation have loomed large in his imagery. It is through this imagery that he called his limitations into being.

How many prayers have ascended heavenward that have contained these words, "Lord, I am not worthy." Our dear ones, it is our desire that you accept for your own those things for which you ask and know that each one of you are of great worth to us and to the heavenly Father. There are none of lesser value or of greater value.

Has it not been said that there are no judgements given by the Father? Those judgements that you feel as worthy or unworthy are self judgements and those judgements by which you measure one another. Has it not come about that when one is wrapped in self guilt, it is easier to say, "my brother has sinned therefore he is lesser than I," than to say, "we neither have sinned, we have only become lost in the darkness and we know not the way." When one does pass judgement of right or wrong upon self, it is easy to see those same issues of right or wrong in those entities about him and man does pass those self same judgements to those outside of self. Would it not be unbearable to see only oneself in a state of sin? Therefore you must look for sins in those about you for if you are unworthy, then those about you must be unworthy also to justify that unworthiness in self.

However, our friends, we repeat, there is no lesser and no greater. You are each of immense beauty and value. You are each a divine being of light, but you see it not. You have only to release those feelings of unworthiness and sin and you are free! Free of all bondage! Give that love and approval to self that you would give to an innocent loving child of your own. You are equally deserving of love and approval. You are equally free of sin and a magnificent shield of light. Forgive self all pain, blame and guilt that you have put upon self. Forgive self and welcome a new and loving vision of self. Keep this imagery of self alive day and night for this is that simple step that man needs to take to free himself of self condemnation and limitation.

The universe gives to you that which you in the deepest most secret part of self do feel worthy or unworthy of receiving, including those strong all encompassing fears that manifest.

One entity may have a very strong core belief in security. It is difficult to get enough of the physical goods of the world together to keep one's body and soul together. A belief pattern of this type results in the manifestation of scarcity in the life of the individual. The belief in scarcity may further be reinforced by a feeling of unworthiness. He may also feel that the worldly goods that he does acquire takes from those who are equally needy. In this case the feelings of scarcity and unworthiness are reinforced by feelings of guilt, and should this entity actually manage to manifest a certain amount of physical goods for his own use, the guilt may manifest in his careless handling of his worldly goods and letting it slip through his fingers, or he may leave it laying about where it will surely be picked up, or in some cases, his guilt may be so great that he may give whatever he may have manifested to someone he deems more worthy than he.

Do you not know that you and you alone are in control of your own little universe that surrounds you? That you are the creator, the director and the leading actor in the play that you find yourself in? Also, by your frame of mind you attract to yourself those entities that play the leading roles as well as those who play the villain? You, my friends, do set the stage. Since you are the director of your play, you may change the lines or the characters taking part in the play at any time that you may choose. Since you also write the script, your play may be a comedy, a tragedy, or a story of the teaching of love and divinity within humanity.

We suggest that should you like to change your life, that you ponder upon these things. Know that you are never alone, that what you earnestly desire and feel worthy of receiving you shall receive.

Choose wisely!

Divinity

One of the greatest gifts given by the Source is divine perfection, and it is part of your being, a law of the universe, a gift that cannot be taken from one entity, but can, and is, often ignored or unrecognized.

The knowledge of your own divinity is the most wonderful shining gift that any one can possibly give to those about him. Accepting your divinity contributes to the perfection and light of the planet. Just the acceptance of that loving gift from Source bestowed at your inception makes it all so very simple yet all mankind has felt the need to make it difficult, to make it a struggle. It is your true state of being whether you accept or deny it and you may manifest as many things or situations as you chose to prove that you are not of divine perfection.

You may become very creative about those manifestations, still it does not change one single thing, it only changes the appearance of what is. Once you do accept that divine perfection as your own energy, you do draw those entities around you into a more accepting state of their own perfection and allows them to see themselves as beings of light and to release some of those self imposed limitations.

The old belief patterns tell us that enlightenment must be difficult, the path strewn with suffering, you must fall and stumble and bruise yourselves. This old programming comes to the surface. So in your illusion of how things must be, you accept the responsibility to manifest those things in your lives that will make it as hard and as painful as you believe it should be. You begin by putting monumental road blocks in your way. You're unworthy, you are limited, there is much to fear, life is hard, you cannot trust yourselves or others, furthermore you cannot trust the divine Source. You on the earthly plane could make a list a mile long. Not only could but frequently do. You who are such consummate creative sinners, how could you accept a magnificent gift of perfection such as the Source has given?

Also there are the few, that should one announce himself to be a divine entity of perfection, there would be a multitude of reactions from the masses, most of them unflattering. However, one does not need to announce his divinity and perfection with a fanfare of trumpets unless that one feels a need to punish, feed the ego, or bring abuse to self. All that is required is to go out into the world quietly and simply be.

Give that great love that your heart is so capable of giving to self. There is not one, not one, who is more deserving of your love than self. Love of self and unconditional acceptance of self just as you are at this time, can and will manifest great changes in you, in your life and finally in those about you. There is no greater gift you can give to self than to love self. To each entity on this planet we would say: you are each of great light and beauty, more than you ever suspect.

Belief Systems

We are with you this day, and we will guide your footsteps all through the day. We are part of you, yet separate, and we do come from the same energy Source. This is the way for all entities upon the earth plane, we and all humanity have the same Source from whence we receive our energy. It is the choice of each separate entity how they will use this energy. And the choice is dependent upon their growth pattern and where they are on the road to self-evolvement.

The Source is energy, energy is love and one who knows himself to be part of the Source, knows himself to have been created from that very same energy, love. All that the Source does create is created by that same love energy. There is a longing of each entity that feels a great emptiness within. The longing for that forgotten time when they knew they were a part of that great loving Source energy, the awareness that they were truly a child of the Father and all that the Father possessed was theirs also. This is the great longing of all mankind, to be aware of that great all encompassing love that they once knew. It can be likened to a desire to return to the womb where there was warmth and protection and nothing was asked except to be and to grow.

Many of those desiring a return to the Father are lost in their self created unreality, and they know not what that great loneliness and longing within their core being is trying to call forth. They are truly lost in darkness, know not that for which they search and for which they long.

At this time when our energies draw near to the earth it is to help each one come face to face with his own identity, to recognize self as a divine entity of light.

Through many lifetimes each entity has grown and evolved in their perceptions of the whole universe, some much faster than others and some have had fewer lifetimes on this earth plane.

In terms of mass consciousness the greater part of humanity views his growth from a perception of right or wrong, and in so doing judges his neighbors' growth by the same yardstick, right or wrong. Well initiate, there is not a right or wrong. There are only many different ways in using the universal energy that is available to all. It can be used for the growth and benefit of mankind as well as the individual. It depends on that perception of right or wrong that the entity, or entities, using the available energy holds at the time of the manifesting. Though we are each of the same Source of energy we each do have free choice of how we shall use the available energy.

Each entity manifests in his life that which he holds to be true in his belief system. As his belief system changes, so do those things that he manifests in the physical change.

Groups who hold the same belief system manifest events in their lives that encompass their belief system. They often band together in clubs, communities, churches, government, etc. If those manifestations come forth from feelings of love for one another it can become a very beneficial experience for the group. If it comes forth from fear, it can be very destructive. Love and fear cannot exist in the same space at the same time. Love is the most powerful energy in the universe. Fear is that distortion of love brought forth through a distorted belief system that labels one thing good and another bad. It gains its power from the energy sent forth from those entities who are held in a vise-like grip of a belief system that invokes fear.

Their belief system is distorted, and their reactions to each other and to life as whole are governed by fear. This fear does cripple and hold each one in its grip. It does overshadow them like a dark cloud. Eventually fear causes blind panic and those entities caught in its grip do manifest from panic. They see and feel most entities as enemies and may be driven to destroy, using either mental, emotional or physical control of others to control their lives. These entities have by their own fear cut themselves off from the Father and the Light.

Guidance

My Dear Ones, when things are so easy, why do you feel compelled to make them so hard? Why must you overlook your strength and your wisdom? You have so much, you have come so far. You must know what happens when you continually downplay your own wonderful qualities. You sell yourself on this point of view, those around you accept this as the true picture, and begin to treat you as though it were indeed a fact, that you are a helpless entity with little or no wisdom or power.

In truth you know this is not a true picture of who you are, but as the feedback coincides with the picture of yourself that you are projecting outward, you become deeply immersed in the feelings that tell you you are less than alright and the hole becomes deeper and deeper and the illusion greater and greater. Now you must consider if this is truly what you want. But may we suggest that you take a good thoughtful look at what you do want. We have much love for you and we are truly with you but you remain in free will at all times. No one can take that from you. With each small decision you take a step in some direction and you are free to choose that direction you will take right or left.

You at times revert back to the poor helpless victim and

you need to be on guard against this. When you accept the role of victim you abdicate all responsibility for manifesting those things in your life with which you are not comfortable and would rather not have. At times you feel like confessing what a really bad person you have been and this is equally destructive to your spiritual growth. We shall aid you in keeping on the path and when you stumble, we shall pick you up.

1. Become a self empowered entity of light. Capable of giving unconditional love, first to self and secondly to those about you for you cannot give to others that which you do not give to self.

2. Accept self as a strong empowered being for that is what you are. You are no longer the helpless confused entity that you perceived yourself to be. That perception is no longer useful to you.

3. Be willing to accept the guidance that you receive from your loving unseen friends from day to day, from hour to hour and from minute to minute. Know that you are not at any time without guidance but that when you put your focus on fear the guidance is blocked, and the fear looms like a black all consuming monster.

4.   Change your focus in thinking. Focus on strength instead of weakness, on success instead of failure. Do not surround your daily interactions with those expectations that things or relationships must turn out this way or that way.

In so doing, you limit self in what you can have. That those with whom you have relationships must relate in certain set patterns, or ways, to fulfill your expectations. In so doing, you put limits on those entities also. This is a particularly difficult lesson for you, since to release all expectations of how relationships in your life must turn out, means that you must relinquish the old need to control.

You know better than the Source, your teachers and guides, or those individuals you are relating to. In the case of the individuals, you know better than they how they should be feeling, relating and so on. To have such expectations is to put severe limits on self, on others, and on what each may have.

As you change and grow, the expectations as to what you may have change and grow. However, through your expectations, you may be asking for a half piece of cake when in fact you could have a whole piece, or maybe a whole cake of your own if you would but open to receive it. It is a point of truth that you put expectations on yourselves and limit them by what you are able to accept. Also, by putting expectations upon others you limit the possibilities of what they may be prepared to give.

True, each entity does have free will, but many times those in a relationship intuit what is expected of them and that is what they give, whether it be wrath or love. This method of putting expectations forth is a way many entities devise to try and avert rejection, deep hurt and abandonment. It is a method to avoid any happenings that might precipitate disappointment or surprises. In the past you have found it so much safer to stay in a nice deep rut. But then you do not go any place, and do not grow. It only keeps you from reaching your full potential. To be able to relinquish all control and expectations and turn things over to the universe is to open up vast possibilities, possibilities that you cannot even envision.

One place that fear, disappointment and hurt have a tendency to creep in, is when there is an attempt to relinquish all control. If one is expressing in a spirit of unconditional love, the results must always be for the very highest good of the individuals involved.

Sometimes this thought that the results will be for the highest good of the individual may be frightening. In truth, it may be a lesson, but all lessons need not be painful, most of the pain is brought into being when there is strong resistance to learning the needed lesson. It is truly possible to welcome the learning experience and to say, "Ah, yes! This is what I have been missing, this little lesson that points out the truth, that I need to accept the pain," if there is pain. Let it go and you are one step farther down the road to self growth, on to better relationships, and the path to enlightenment.

Love

Know that we are with you each hour of the day and the night. We hear each request that you make and each request is granted. We do not sit in judgement on those requests, say that you may have this yet you may not have that. We do not make choices for one single entity upon the earth. We would not be allowed to do so even if we chose to, and we do not so choose.

It is our desire to foster your growth by surrounding you with our loving energy, acknowledging your divinity and your free will at all times.

We are all working with the energy of the universe and the energy we are speaking of is love, the most powerful and abundant energy of the universe. Yet in your earth plane you sometimes use it so sparingly that it would seem a scarce commodity, and would possibly deplete the whole supply at any moment. Is this not a most unusual conception? How can one deplete the very substance from which the universe and all within the universe was created? Be as extravagant with love as you please. Fling it about with abandon and great joy, for it is one energy that does not harm. It only heals, brings peace and joy. Know that whatever love you give to others, to the earth, to the universe, comes back to you for love begets love.

So why all of this fear to give love? Fear of rejection you may say! How can you receive rejection from love? A gift of love? Only when love is not truly love but a hidden request for something in return can you receive rejection. When there is an unspoken request in the giving of love, it is not a gift but a hidden demand and it says that one must give me something in return. This is a conception of love that is within the mass consciousness.

When an entity does give love they must be deeply honest about their motives. Are they truly giving love or are they asking in a hidden way for something? When we speak of love, we speak of unconditional love, love given without any hidden request, not an expectation that the love or something else be returned to the giver, for that is not a gift it is a request for an exchange. And when it is put forth in a hidden manner it is an attempt to manipulate and control.

There are, at times, perfectly legitimate requests are made between two entities, but they should be put forth openly and honestly as a request, for one can request one's help, one's support, or even one's love but it should be put forth as a request not a gift.

Love, Self Love

Our dear ones, we would say again that the most beautiful gift one can give to self is the gift of self love. Loving and forgiving self each mistake and loving and accepting self in each success. Why should the love for self falter when one stumbles? Does faltering or soaring make one entity more worthy or less worthy than another?

Who is to say one's contribution is greater than another? By whose yardstick do you measure these things? The Father in Heaven does not create a scale by which he grades his beloved children as more worthy, less worthy, or completely unworthy. With the Father, there is no measuring of one against the other. There are no greater and no lesser. There are only those who walk different paths to learn the same lessons, which they need to learn to bring self to light and wisdom.

If the Father does not condemn one for his omissions, who among you is willing to do so? Is one truly guilty of failure or merely guilty of failing to live up to his own expectations, or the expectations of parents, teachers, friends, neighbors, churches, government and state?

From the time of infancy each entity is saddled with many expectations from outside of self. Therefore, with so many outside expectations he then loses touch with self. Parents and those beings who are entrusted with the care of a small child have the responsibility to love, care for and guide them. But who gives them the right to heap expectations upon them, tell them what path they must walk, that they must achieve excellence in this or that, or that they must follow the teachings of this church or this group, or that they must excel in order to bring glory and a feeling of pride and accomplishment to the parent?

The threat of failure brings guilt to those small ones growing up in this atmosphere and the guilt erodes the self-confidence and the feelings of self worth. The Heavenly Father gives us our own free will to choose. Each entity must choose his own path and the more freedom of choice they are given by those earthly parents, the less guilt they may feel if they sometimes stumble and do not achieve those objectives they set for themselves to please the parents.

Each one does make mistakes no matter which path he may choose. When these mistakes are evaluated with an open mind and heart, they are stepping stones to wisdom. Each lesson learned allows one to take a step upward, toward that divinity and that light which are his natural state, but he knows it not as yet.

We see those among you who are buried in self condemnation. Their expectations of self or the expectations of others for them are so high there is always that feeling of failure, of not being enough, the inability to achieve those high goals. And what does self condemnation net the individual? More failure, less self-esteem and more self condemnation.

Heaping condemnations upon self can become a spiral downward, self value is eroded away, and self condemnation becomes a means of self punishment. Self punishment attracts those who would be abusive in their relationships. The self condemnation and the abuse becomes a means of manifesting those feelings of unworthiness. It is as if they have this need to tell the world how truly unworthy they are. The prisons are full of these entities who have been blinded to their true identity and are seemingly lost in darkness. This cycle continues until something or someone causes these entities to recognize who they truly are, entities of light and divinity, and to recognize they are of great value.

Sometimes it takes much energy from outside to help change this self destructive image, and it is appropriate to use those means provided by God through another. One who has healed himself of those destructive self images may come into the presence of those lost ones and give love and support freely without getting caught in the game of returning abuse for abuse. To heal oneself is to know one is totally free of "error," to know they are a shining, loving human being of great value and without flaws. That this shining perfection is a gift of the Father and they have never lost this gift, only for a time forgotten who they were. So only by accepting our own perfection can we heal ourselves and eventually help those around us.

Jesus healed himself thus: by recognizing and claiming his own perfection. He was the greatest psychiatrist that walked upon earth and by healing himself he freed himself of all self-imposed limitations, went forth, and by reflecting his perfection and love outward to those who came to him, they were then able to heal themselves.

This is the meaning of enlightenment. To return to that awareness where one is in a state of light, and to know one's own perfection. He recognizes that that state of perfection was always there, but lost in illusion.

Love, Belief Patterns

There is a great wave of light breaking over the earth like a glorious sunrise. It is lighting the hearts and minds of those who open themselves to receive it. It is like the sound of an angelic choir trembling in wondrous harmony. As the light breaks, man awakens from the deep sleep that he has called upon himself. All creation will truly know who and what man is. The lion and the lamb (also symbolizing the inner natures of man that war one with the other), will again lie down together in harmony. For as the consciousness of man changes, so does this bring about change within the natures of those creatures about him, for we are all one, living in one great pool of cosmic consciousness.

Each entity that is awakened from his sleep becomes aware of the opening of his heart center and this great swell of love from the Father that extends outward to all those upon the earth plane. One must first love oneself; then extend that love outward to all things. In this way all things will be healed, for love is and always has been the great healer, the wonderful energy that opens the heart, the mind and frees one from that veil of illusion.

It must be kept in mind that many entities may have one outer belief system which they wear like a cloak, and a much deeper more firmly ingrained system within. This inner belief system is the one that has been programmed for many eons of time by the mass consciousness, by parents, teachers, friends, lovers, and many other sources. Some of the programming has been found invalid and dropped away, some seemed safe and worthy of keeping. These patterns have their affect on the belief system of every single individual in the earth plane. Sometimes an individual may discover that a belief pattern is not valid at this time in his life. During the life time or life times of any given entity, the belief system may be altered many times and each time the core belief is altered, the corresponding manifestation in the life of the entity is altered. For some entities, though they may be in the minority, who believe the path to enlightenment is a joyous, glorious one, filled with love, light and without need for suffering tremendous trauma or pain along the way. What each entity believes and expects in the very core of his being will faithfully be brought into manifestation.

Christ did recognize that he and the Father were one, not only intellectually but from within his being and so was able to throw off those limitations that all mankind has imposed upon self. The lack of recognition of one's Christ awareness, stands in the way of many entities assuming their full power and going beyond the illusion of limitations.

Love

At this time many of us draw near to the earth so that our energies may be felt by those upon the planet. We send forth energies of love and hope in the light rays that emanate from our hearts. It is our desire to plant the seed of love in the hearts of many. It is the choice of each entity to water and nourish the seed and let it come forth in abundance, or to leave the seed in darkness, without benefit of nourishment where it will wither and die. It is a choice each one shall make.

We see many beautiful beings on the earth plane who have love radiating forth from their harts in colorful rays of light and it is a magnificent sight to behold. Yet there are many who are in darkness or near darkness. At this time in the earth's evolution it is important that the light of love be anchored in the hearts of many that all may have an opportunity to experience the light and love from the light beings on high who now draw near. It is our desire that many may accept our gift of light into their bodies where it will increase abundantly and be given out again from one to another. Thus the vibration of the earth may be raised into a higher plane where man's inhumanity to man may cease and be replaced by loving, giving, and receiving from one to another. This is our desire, not only for all humanity but for the earth itself that man's abuse of the earth may cease and that it may be replaced by the role of caretaker.

We from on high see the darkness and the pain, and, yes, even the grief that resides in your hearts. We see the slow and helpless movements of your body, and the heaviness of your steps, and we now draw near to heal the hearts that are filled with self hate. We project the energy of love and light in even higher voltage so that you may feel and know our presence is near, for now is the time of your opening. We are all part of the Source and part of one another.

When there is love in the hearts of man it helps to heal the hearts of others. Where there is darkness and a festering sore it has an affect on the cells and the health of those cells about them. You are all parts of the whole and we seek to help the whole become healed.

Thus we send those energies of love and light through all who will receive. In this way those who accept the love and light shall love self and heal self. Each one who is healed shall have an affect on the healing of those about them, and the healing shall radiate outward in ever widening circles.

Love and Forgiveness

We would ask you to remember that love and forgiveness can overcome all difficulties, that loving self can truly heal self in every way. That in loving others you extend the energy that makes it possible for those bathed in the radiance of your love to feel themselves as loved, then they also can learn to give love to self and in this way enter upon the path to self-healing.

It is so simple, yet humanity has for eons of time made it so difficult for self and for others. When all trappings are stripped away, at the core of each individual is that great longing to be loved, not knowing they are already loved, by their Heavenly Father, or the Source. When there is such longing for that healing energy of love, why is it that it is so cautiously and so sparingly given? When there is such longing why is it so cautiously received?

To understand and accept one's fears and to know from whence they came is a step toward healing and releasing the fear. If the fear is denied and suppressed it holds the fear within the body and returns over and over like a tape repeating itself. To accept the fear, allow self to feel the fear and to understand it is a step toward releasing it and releasing the need to replay the tape. This at times takes great courage. No one is eager to look fear in the eye, but is it not worth it to find self? It is a tremendous load lifted from the heart.

Love and Healing

We would say a few words concerning using the healing energy of love in negotiations, whether it be at the peace table, or the dinner table. The healing takes place when each entity present lays aside his own personal desire to be right, to benefit at the expense of others, to elevate their ego by condemning, denouncing, or belittling another to whatever degree. None of the above belong at the negotiation table.

Winning takes place when all of those present, caught by the spirit of healing, love and cooperation, come forth from the negotiations feeling more self love and self approval, not less. Seldom does one feel inclined to concede a little here or there to one who, in however a subtle way, caused them to have a loss of self-esteem or self love.

There is also a second ingredient that must be present at the negotiation table and that ingredient is faith. For successful negotiations one must have faith in those with whom he is negotiating. If one comes in faith he will be received in faith. If one comes in a state of suspicion, he will be received with suspicion.

Always - *like attracts like.* When dealing with entities and hoping for a mutually unified agreement the approach of how much can I reasonably give, never how much can I take, is a powerful approach. This does not mean to open oneself to be taken unfair advantage by another, or to take or accept any abuse from another. These negotiations need to come from a strong sense of self love and self integrity. Self integrity and self love surrounds one with an energy that does not allow being taken advantage of either mentally, emotionally, or physically.

Change, Patterns, Peace

We would speak to you of those difficult times ahead when many adjustments will be made, by individuals and by mankind as a whole. There are many opportunities that those on the earth plane are given to learn. It need not be difficult and painful unless those receiving the opportunities chose to make it so. Those individuals who cannot accept change and let go of past ways of thinking, or not thinking, may find it difficult indeed. One must let go of worn out thought patterns and ways of reacting before growth can take place, growth is change. In these coming times of rapid change, some may accept this as an opportunity and an adventure and others accept it as a hardship.

Each individual does make a choice. It will be an opportunity to come into tune with the earth, and for all mankind upon the earth to come into harmony, one with the other. If there is not harmony in an individual he will not come into harmony with his brother. If one is in harmony with the self, it will flow in an imperceptible way outward to others, and so over the earth.

It is most urgent that all mankind become aware of the need for peace on this planet, that this great and beautiful planet earth may be blessed and returned to peace that it may heal itself and be able to sustain those billions of entities upon it. Also in these coming times it must be restored to its former brilliance.

Each one upon the planet will have those opportunities to help self, others about them and the planet to be restored to peace and light.

It is our hope that each one of you upon the planet accept these changes as opportunities and challenges and may help others to see these changes you each make in your life and so be challenged to make those changes in their own way of thinking and relating to all things. If this be so, then there need not be those tremendous upheavals to get the attention of those upon the planet. Each one must begin by living and healing self and accepting his neighbor in a non-judgmental and loving way. All those upon the planet are asked to lay down the sword and accept the olive branch. Peace will not come about through violence. Violence does beget violence. We ask all of those who have ears to hear to join the ranks of the peacemakers.

You upon the earth can no longer think in exclusive terms. The sun, moon, stars and the rain are not exclusive gifts to be enjoyed and the pleasure of a few only. Nor are love, nurturing, abundance and peace exclusive. We ask you to be inclusive with all of the above, and if you are including all humanity in love, your desire for peace and abundance, you will be prompted from the heart to do something about it. Do whatever your heart tells you to do, it may be a small thing at first, but there is not one upon the planet who cannot reach out in love and peace to one another. Do you not see what a vast difference that could make?

Always when one takes an exclusive stance, he robs himself of the opportunity and pleasure of extending his own growth and understanding. You on this planet cannot afford to love only the Christian, the Jew, the Hindus or any exclusive group or religion. By doing so you limit your own growth and ability to give and you deprive others of your love and understanding that may have raised them to a higher place of understanding and ability to give. If you lift those limitations and think and act in all inclusive terms you make room for love, light, cooperation and peace to come into the world. It can begin with one and that one can be you.

The practice of exclusiveness was not at any time appropriate, it has pitted one group against another, one nation against another and one religion against another. At this time, it is imperative that this be resolved so that the planet and those upon it may survive. You may begin now in some small way or you may continue on your set way of thinking and wait until some painful learning experience catapults you into the realization that change is necessary.

You, our dear ones do make the choice, no one can choose for you. If you would but open your eyes and the door to your heart, you would know that all, be it Christian, Jew, Pagan, Hindu or Muslim, are on the same path and that is the path back to the Source of all things by whatever name you may choose to designate. The path you have chosen makes no difference since they all, all lead to the one central light. Is the belief system that one chooses his path to the light, or the name that one chooses to give the Source of all things worth spilling the blood of countless ones? Is it worth attracting countless numbers of painful learning experiences to oneself? There can be a diversity of opinion and a unity of purpose, and a loving acceptance of those with diverse opinions.

Our dear ones, the path to God is so simple yet mankind makes it so difficult. All humanity is crying out from that great central need in each one, the desperate desire to be loved and accepted as they are. Then why is it so difficult to give and receive with each other simply because the path you have chosen is not labeled by the same name? Do you not know that all roads lead to Damascus? Do you not know the path to peace is a very simple one, love your brother as yourself? And one must love self before he can love his brother. It is the inner self that needs healing before one can love another.

There have been many teachers sent forth down through time and they have taught in many different languages for would it not be foolish to send a teacher forth to teach in a language that is not understood by those he was teaching? However, the core of the message has always been the same, love and forgiveness. All else has been added to or subtracted from the central messages, and each group or religion has added their own interpretation according to their belief system. It is now time to return to the central message which can be accepted by all. The message of love and forgiveness. It is so very simple yet mankind has managed to complicate it beyond recognition. This is the message that can bind people together instead of separating one from another. Only by a unity of purpose can the earth be healed and those upon the earth be healed.

Nothing, nothing is set in concrete, all things ebb and flow. Truly change is the road to growth and we would ask you to consider growing in peace. It is as though you were a camera, seeing the world through a very narrow lens opening, and we ask you to use your wide-angle lens and allow a much wider perspective to enter into your consciousness.

Energies, Change

We would speak to you of those energies many of you are experiencing at this time. These energies that are at this time coming into the earth plane, the purpose of these energies is to precipitate change and those who can accept change will flow more easily than those who stubbornly resist change. We say to you that to stand still and resist change is detrimental to the individual, the governing systems, the monetary systems and the earth itself. For where there is not change there cannot be growth.

All energy is motion and where energy ceases to flow there is deterioration. There has been great resistance in certain areas on this planet earth. Man may look about him to see deterioration in the monetary system, the governing bodies, in individual lives and in some instances, one country's approach to another where there has been a steadfast refusal to change.

Because of the deterioration in many of the financial institutions and many of the governing bodies there may be a widespread reorganization of the monetary systems and many of the governing bodies.

But first there will be felt by some, those painful lessons. There may be those who will lose much of worldly goods and those who may be unable to meet their financial obligations. There have been rumblings of this for some time, yet many have not listened. The spending on various parts of the planet has been rampant without consideration of the affect this may have upon the monetary systems of the world. This has been done in the name of many different motives, yet the underlying motive is greed.

Those who have an imbalance in their lives will be in a position where they must recognize this imbalance and alter their belief patterns to reflect the truth. Just as there must be a balance of breathing in and breathing out, there is a balance of the coming and going of the tides, where there is imbalance there is potential destruction. There will be some difficult lessons learned. It is best that those with awareness to do so prepare themselves and bring balance into their own lives in the realm of finances. To allow fear and panic to manifest will bring those things most feared into being. Those who have eyes to see and ears to hear will neither fear nor panic, but will make those changes toward balance and harmony. Balance, that great law of the universe.

Each entity draws to himself those lessons most needed at any given time. If one in his most hidden thoughts feels he can learn only by rather harsh means, he will attract those harsh situations to self. The harshness of the lesson depends on the ability of the entity to listen to those messages that are received, and the more quickly acted upon and learned, the sooner the lesson is completed. It is at all times a choice of the individual. Some learn more quickly than others.

Those entities whose self-esteem and self worth is directly tied to material possessions, many find it difficult indeed. More difficult than those who have become aware that self worth is that which comes from within and has been since his creation, rather than a reflection of that which are his material possessions. Those material things that contribute to health, comfort, growth, beauty and that nourish the spirit are indeed desirable for all. It is only where there is an inappropriate balance of those energies that there is a need to restructure one's thinking and actions to bring things into balance once again. When the identity is very closely identified with those material things one owns and there is a loss of those material goods, there is also a loss of the personal identity and a loss of self worth. This frequently precipitates a crisis. Through the crisis, some may suddenly find their real strength and their inner sense of worthiness while others may experience powerlessness.

Our dear ones, we say to you, think on these things and make those choices that are appropriate for you to live with, for thus it will be. For some who have allowed the imbalance to become very great, it is our hope and desire that they may find the strength and the willingness to make those changes that must be made to bring their lives into balance.

Forgiveness

We would speak to you on forgiving self for what you term mistakes in your lives, when you have taken an apparent detour or a wrong turn in your path. From time to time each and all make what appears to be inappropriate decisions or inappropriate actions.

When putting a picture puzzle together you sometimes try the wrong piece and when it isn't a good fit you remove it and try another without any sense of failure or self condemnation. When this happens in your life and you term it a mistake, why is it so difficult to forgive yourself, release it, and go on; why must one cling to a sense of guilt, a sense of failure? A sense of self condemnation for years, maybe a lifetime because of trying out a way of reaction or an action that you discovered later appeared to be inappropriate for that time and place?

Is it a commentary on your self worth or you as a success or a failure? Or is it a misperception of what may have been an appropriate action/reaction at that time? Is it not possible to recognize the action or reaction as inappropriate, take responsibility for it, bless it and release it?

When one is attached to a constant remembrance of certain so called past mistakes, it lives on in the body and memory of that entity and ties it in a very real way to the past. These memories prevent an entity from going forward vigorously and joyously to create a better future with the knowledge gained from the past mistakes. When there is an attachment to these mistakes they lodge in the body and cause the one in which they are stuck to become more tense with less movement of energy. Eventually, the density within the body causes an aberration which results in a disease in that affected area.

Once the lesson has been learned there is nothing to be gained by an attachment to past mistakes and it does slow the progress of the entity involved. Is it not better to accept self at this very minute for what you are now, not yesterday, not tomorrow, but today? Accept self for what you are now. Wipe the slate clean and go from there.

If a gifted artist makes a mistake on a beautiful masterpiece that is being painted, and then for days, months and years is in a state of self remorse, condemnation, guilt and anger, the masterpiece would never come forth. When in truth, all that was needed was to paint over the mistake on the canvas (release the mistake) and proceed with the bringing forth of the masterpiece as if the mistake had not been made. Now the artist did learn that a certain technique or shade of coloring did not work under these particular circumstances. So, therefore, he gained some knowledge for future reference and there was no loss in the mistake.

All life and all learning is change. By refusing to release the mistakes of the past, one fails to learn from them and one is unable to accept change, so there is no growth for the future. Each one upon the planet is in the process of painting a masterpiece; a masterpiece that is the self. Many times you may need to paint over the mistakes upon the canvas, but you are bringing forth a masterpiece and it is your gift to the Lord of the universe. We are all in a state of becoming and forever will be in a state of becoming, there is no standing still. A state of becoming means a state of change.

Giving And Receiving

Now we would give you some thoughts on giving and receiving. They are closely related, there are those entities that have much difficulty in receiving. There is that popular conception that it is more worthy to give than to receive. Truly, they are part of the same thing for there cannot be a giving without a receiving.

There are those who feel that by giving, they have earned a right to feel worthy. Worthiness is not something that can be earned, nor do we, your teachers and guides, request or desire any sacrifice from any individual in order for them to achieve worthiness. Worthiness is that which you are, you always have been and you always shall be. Giving does not make you more worthy or less worthy. Giving is an act of extending love from one entity to another. It is a tremendously beneficial act both to the giver and to the receiver.

To extend oneself in love to another increases the love and the pleasure in the heart of the giver and the receiver. Giving does not at any time, if given in the spirit of love and asking nothing in return, deplete the giver. Giving in the spirit of love is expanding one's capacity to love unconditionally.

Receiving the gift, given in a state of love also expands the capacity of the receiver. It is an open flowing of the energy of love. If one entity chooses not to receive, the flow of love is not complete. That opportunity for opening the heart of the receiver and expanding its love capacity is lost, and there is a withholding on the part of the receiver. This causes the energy to slow its movement and density forms in the body of the receiver's heart area. It stops there until the receiver chooses to open the heart area and allow expansion to take place.

Now, if the gift of the giver is refused and the giver is a well balanced, centered individual, there is no change in that inner flow of love, the love still flows to the intended receiver even though the gift was not accepted and the giver still feels an expansion. However, if the giver is still working on becoming a balanced entity and his ego is easily threatened, there may be a shutting down in the heart area and a slowing of the energy and the giver then feels the refusal as a comment on his own worthiness.

In truth, it is merely a comment on how the receiver is at that time feeling about self. Perhaps at that time he may have been feeling himself as unworthy of receiving that gift. We would say again that worthiness is not something that one can earn, something that one can become. Worthiness is that which you are. It may take an entity many lifetimes to recognize this. It may be recognized by some at one time and then lost again in the dim memory of the past.

Some entities may feel they have committed such unspeakable crimes that they have lost that right to worthiness. In the process of learning who they are there are those also who may have indeed been lost to the light and committed those crimes that were not appropriate and that were truly not acceptable to self and to society. Their sense of self esteem and sense of worthiness may have been injured and they suffered a very painful experience and the suffering may have extended over a period of time. But one must remember that this was a choice to learn by a painful lesson. It was all a learning experience that one may grow into a higher realm of knowledge. Perhaps the lesson may have been learned in a less painful fashion, but again it was a matter of choice.

Those in the higher realms feel love and compassion for those who are suffering. It is man who is hard on self and it is man who is judgmental and hard on man.

In the human family one member metes out very harsh punishment to his fellow brothers. If one is feeling a need for severe punishment he will in turn sentence another to a very severe punishment. It is for this reason that we who are your brothers ask you to accept that divinity which is your own, to love and honor self and at all times, accept self as one of great worth, for truly you are.

We also ask that there may be a joyful giving and receiving within the human family. A great giving and receiving of love and those gifts of the spirit, that you each may take advantage of this simple and easy path to growth. It involves no pain. We ask you to be gentle with self, to be forgiving with self, to release that mistaken belief in sin. How many times and how many ways have we said to you; there is not any sin? There is only that illusion of sin in the mind of man to which he clings. Those illusions born of mass programming, programming by those in authority, unreal expectations of self and others, and faulty perceptions.

Now we would ask, who are those in authority over self? There are many different answers that have been given but who is the true authority over self? There is no higher authority over man than that very true essence of man, the God Self. All final decisions for each individual must be made by that divine core, the God Self. Therein lies the responsibility for each individual.

Everywhere man is in pain. The pain that is manifested on this planet is sorry to behold. Yet we can say to you that when man no longer feels the need for pain, he will not manifest those situations that are painful to him. It was not, at any time decreed by God, that man should suffer and draw pain to self. When the guilt is completely released, one has forgiven self for the guilt and the guilt is healed, the need for pain will also be healed. Man will then cease to create those situations that cause him pain.

These illusions that alter the mind of man are born of the mind and they can be released by the mind, by making that choice to do so.

This also includes the need for illness, aging, and death. We would say to you, this will come our dear ones. Change is coming rapidly. The powerful love energy that is now being released upon the earth by those great loving beings of light from on high will have its affect.

Faith

When you ask in faith, you receive in love. Faith is that state of consciousness when there is a deep and abiding knowing from within, all doubt has been put aside, all feeling of unworthiness and guilt released. It is that inner knowing that what is desired shall be received. And one stands in faith.

When one walks in faith his heart opens to the healing love of the Father. When an entity accepts, willingly and wholeheartedly the love from the Father, there is that wonderful filling of the empty space in the heart center, a sense of divine exaltation that has to be felt to be known. Man does in that moment of faith accept the Father as a totally loving and giving Father, and releases all thoughts of punishment, loss of love, and unworthiness.

In the unconsciousness of most of humanity on the planet earth, there is often the projection of the qualities and characteristics of the earthly father upon the Heavenly Father. An entity, who has experienced condemnation from the earthly father, subconsciously perceives the possibility of the same condemnation coming forth from the Heavenly Father. This is indeed an illusion but much of humanity's present belief system is based upon illusion.

This not only increases the feeling of unworthiness and powerlessness but it blocks the path to faith and the receiving of the ever present love from the heavenly Father. It blocks the ability of that one to receive that which he most desires and for which he has asked.

God is the very essence of love and could not be otherwise. Man, who came forth a divine spark from the essence of God also cannot be otherwise, but man knows it not as he is blinded by his own doubt and lack of faith. In his blindness to his own divinity and his own perfection, he has cut himself off from the light, which is love and is there to sustain him at all times.

The more deeply man becomes separated from his true identity, the less he is able to receive the light, and as his body becomes more dense, he receives even less light. The separation was not at any time that God did not recognize man as his own, but rather that man did not recognize and accept God as the loving Father.

In this path of illusion, mankind has attracted darkness to himself. In this state of darkness, density and feelings of powerlessness, man does feel that God does not recognize him and does not hear or respond to his petitions. Therefore, he, mankind, must have committed some grievous sin and is unworthy of that which all mankind so fervently desires, love and light from the Heavenly Father. The love and light are at all times given but most of mankind knows it not.

In his illusion of separation from God and loss of His love, mankind in his blindness feels abandoned by God. Rather mankind has abandoned God and in so doing has abandoned self. Man cannot abandon God without abandoning self, for at all times there is that oneness with man and God. How could it be otherwise when man was created of that divine essence of the Source which is pure love? When one feels abandonment there are enormous feelings of unworthiness and guilt. For why would the Heavenly Father from whom all mankind so desires love, abandon him, unless he was truly unworthy of the Father's love? So man in his subconscious, assuming great guilt, does further separate himself from God and assumes responsibility for something that in reality did not take place.

A child when abandoned by a parent does in his subconscious assume the guilt for the act, often feeling he has not lived up to the expectation of the parent. The alternative is to assume the mother or the father to be a bad and unloving parent; this would be even more damaging and frightening to the young child who has not yet developed a firm sense of who he is.

And so it is with those upon earth. To see God as an unworthy Father would cause one to feel even more helpless and hopeless. When mankind does feel unworthy, unloved and guilty, he manifests those things in his life or lives, over and over, to prove that he is unworthy of the Father's love and unworthy to receive those things he so earnestly desires.

So this state of darkness perpetuates itself until each individual who is seeking self understanding, by whatever method, comes to a realization that besides the gift of love, there is a second great gift all mankind has received and like the divine spark of perfection, it is bestowed upon all mankind and remains with humanity through all time and space. This is the gift of free choice.

When an individual becomes aware of free choice he becomes aware of the road to freedom and the ability to release his own bonds. He may begin with one small choice, to forgive self for all the real or imagined sins that he has taken upon self. This is the path that mankind is on and has been on for eons. Progressing sometimes and regressing at others. This is not to say that mankind has not at all times used free choice, for surely he has, but using it in an unconscious way, not aware that all that came into his life experience was manifested by his choice. In many cases it was his choice to give up for a time, or give to another that free choice. It is the assuming of the responsibility to make conscious choices that one needs to do in order to proceed on the path to reclaiming higher thought, that divine perfection in which he came forth, that awareness of the oneness of all things and that accepting of the light which sustains from within.

Faith

Know ye not that we hear before you speak? That we are nearer than your breath? That those things for which you ask are already given? Has it not been said, many times over, that we are one? How then do you doubt? Do you not know within the depth of your being that those things for which you ask are available to you? Has it not been said, many times according to your faith, it shall be done? Have you faith the size of a mustard seed, you shall move mountains.

The missing ingredient is faith, and with the trust of a small child you shall open your hearts and receive. Is this so very difficult? It is this that we ask of you, that you shall have faith that it shall be done.

When your thoughts are upon lack, fear, distrust, unworthiness and discouragement, it is these that you manifest. It is through the energy of your thoughts that you manifest, for thoughts do have energy.

We say to you dear ones, wake up! Too long have you lived in a world of illusion, too long have you been separated from your true essence, your true power. Know that the Lord thy God is with you, is a part of you and did bring you forth in love, beauty, power and that you all are Gods!

Know that the state of divine perfection in which you came forth has not changed one whit.

It was through the lack of trust that fear began to manifest in many different forms. It was the fear that took you into the world of illusion. Fear that you were unworthy, separated from God, came forth in sin, had no power, all of which separated you from the truth and the light. Your world has grown dark indeed. At this time our energies draw near to the earth, we are your brothers from on high and our energies are light.

It is the light that sustains you, dear ones, not the darkness, the darkness is only an illusion that caused you to fall asleep to reality. Now is the time to release those fears and allow the light to manifest within you and to bring liberation. You will know a new reality and a new heaven and a new earth. We ask you to love self, to love one another, to love all creatures and to know that all things are one.

Is this so very difficult? We have come forward to bring love, light, hope and truth into the lives of those who open their hearts to receive these gifts. Know that this is the time of awakening. Know that you came forth as Gods and Gods you still be!

Peace

You are each one here upon this planet for the same purpose, to bring forth a better quality of life for yourselves and your offspring. It is a fact of life that this cannot be accomplished through violence and war. Violence only begets violence, rage begets rage. Not only does war destroy the quality of life upon the earth, it destroys the people and will eventually destroy the planet.

So what good does war bring forth? This military preparedness around the world, this mania to be at war or be prepared for war at a moment's notice has indeed bankrupted the many nations so involved. It has created enough weaponry to blow you off the earth many times over. It has created a problem as to where to store the weaponry as well as a problem as to what to do with the outmoded weaponry. Yet another problem it has created is how to dispose of the tremendous toxic waste generated by this insane madness.

There is no trust among the nations of the earth. There is not that opportunity to look up at the stars and enjoy the peace and serenity of the stars and the planets above. There is not that opportunity to enjoy those things in peaceful coexistence.

You, my friends are a member of the universe, whether or not you took a vote upon it, you just are. You have responsibilities to the other planets and life forms upon them. You are even now polluting the water, polluting the atmosphere, and if you are left to your own devices, through this madness there is a chance that, not only will you render this place earth an unfit place to life, the atmosphere unfit to breath, but also the atmosphere of the universe unfit to sustain life.

So this is what you call guaranteeing each individual the right to live in peace?

We are the citizens of the universe who serve as caretakers of the universe, and we will not permit this to take place! You who are incarnated on the most beautiful of all planets, you who were given an abundance of all things to live in peace, you have been privileged to live upon this majestic planet that could with very little effort and technical knowledge be restored to a most desirable paradise, you will not be allowed to destroy the planet for habitation.

You were given free choice on this one little planet and the caretakers of this planet hoped you would grow up. You may, if you so choose, pollute your air, water and soil so that your offspring may come forth crippled mutants, both mentally and physically. You may bring forth untold misery for yourselves. My citizens of the world, you may bring forth a world disaster of your monetary systems for indeed you are very close to that.

If you would but donate a small portion of that spent upon weaponry to efforts of cleaning up your waste, air, water and in the process restoring health to your land, it could be accomplished in a comparatively short time.

If you employed those brilliant scientific minds incarnated now upon the earth to bring forth scientific information to restore the earth to its former glory, to deal with the toxic waste and purify the land and sea, it could be done without an enormous burden to any one individual or group. All that needs be done is direct some of the flow of energy from preparing for war to preparing for peace. You have the brilliant minds, you have the potential to do so. All that you do not have is the will to do so.

You do not, any of you, trust your neighboring citizenry. How does the entire citizenry of the planet switch from suspicion and distrust to trust and cooperation? By one step at a time, one small act of love. Give that love to yourself. Forgive yourself for any and all of those deeds and thoughts that you consider as being unworthy of your highest aspirations. Forgive self, love self and accept self as a most worthy being of light. When one has found self worthy of love and self acceptance, then will he find those companions worthy of love and acceptance. Then and then only, may you take up the olive branch and go forth with that awareness that one must first have love in his heart to have peace in his heart. We say to you the time is critical, the need for peace is now. First bring peace to your own household, then go forth into the world, holding forth peace as the alternative to war, and to eventual destruction of your own beautiful magnificent planet which has sustained and nurtured you these many eons.

This is the first small step. It is only a candle in the darkness, but from one candle, millions of candles may be lighted, the darkness can be dispelled. Know from the very depth of your being that you do count and then stand up and be counted! Walk for peace, sing for peace, sign for peace, greet even your worst enemy in peace. Make peace such a visible part of your life, your state, your country, that the message speaks with such power that those who are in high places will know that their citizenry demands peace, that peace is foremost in their minds.

We have said you need not be violent, we have not said

you need be silent. Let there not be a silent one among you. Let there be peace in each of your hearts for that which is uppermost in your hearts and your desires will surely manifest in your lives. Let each one of you stand up for peace, let no one be mistaken that you do call for peace. You are the caretakers of this earth. We suggest you assume the responsibilities of caretakers. Demand that this destruction cease.

How many of those figures holding office in high places chose peace first as their slogan? How many? Where did their priorities lie? Where? There were many empty promises made but not one had the courage and integrity to step forth among the masses and say. "I am for peace, I want the arms race to cease! The creation of a multitude of weapons has not, and cannot bring peace. I am for world cooperation." Was there one among your aspiring leaders who had the courage and conviction to speak this way? Where have all the courageous ones gone?

Dear Friends, the time is now, not next week, next month or next year, the time is now! We ask the Citizens, as caretakers of this planet, to come forth in unison and stand up for their true rights for a peaceful coexistence. Be verbal, demand to be heard. Be visible, stand tall to be counted. We ask you, dear earth ones, to grow up, take your responsibility to the planet and to those on the planet seriously. There is nothing to be lost but tremendous benefits to be gained.

If you care not for your own health and welfare, consider those young ones who come after and who will have to bear the burden of your irresponsibility, who will have to pay with their health and their lives. We wish you to think!

Peace cannot come through war, peace cannot come through fear, peace cannot come through force. Peace can come only through those who are at peace within themselves. One who is at war with himself, his family or his fellow man cannot bring peace. The peacemaker is that one who has self love, self acceptance and is at peace with self. From this state of being the peace maker does receive his power, his strength and his direction. He is not influenced by a vested interest in this or that, his eye is single, therefore his purpose is simple. Those entities who come from this state of being are connected to the higher source from that state of the Christ Consciousness and from thence came their power.

Through peace within self, one radiates peace to those who are seeking peace.

Through self love, one does radiate love to his fellow man.

Love and peace are synonymous. We say to you the symbol for peace is not the sword, but the olive branch. When one comes in the guise of seeking peace with sword in hand, it strikes fear and resistance in the heart of the adversary. The reaction of fear mobilizes the energies within the body to attack. When one comes in peace with an olive branch in hand it is disarming. There is no threat therein. We say to you that each person who seeks peace must release that need for control over his fellow man before he takes up the olive branch, to be at peace does not imply control of others. Peace comes through cooperation, not control. Control is power through force rather than power through peace. The power through peace comes from the all encompassing love and compassion that radiates from the heart of one entity to another.

The desire for peace is put aside when desire for power arises. Control over small things leads to control over large things and the desire for even more power, which is a false power. It is a power through force rather than power through peace. Power from within comes from control of one's own thoughts, actions and reactions. Control over another is not acceptable. God did not decree one man should have dominion over another or that one nation should have dominion over another. We say to you that not one entity can, in all good consciousness, seek control of another. Control negates that great gift given by God to mankind, the right to make one's own choices. The God given right to make one's own mistakes and thereby profit. We say to you when you have released the need for power over others and accepted that responsibility for self, you are on the path to peace.

How many times has it been said, "Seek ye first the kingdom of heaven and all else shall be added unto you." That kingdom of heaven is that place within mankind where love and peace do reign supreme. Where the Father and the Son are one. Where there is no split and no separation. Each is part of the whole. Is it so difficult to lay aside all need for violence, all need for control and accept the love, the peace and the protection of the Father? Is this what you would see as a sacrifice? In so doing making way for the innate creativity of each individual to come forth in the creation of a new world order where peace does reign supreme. Is this not the fulfillment the longing and the desire that comes from the heart of each entity?

Abundance

We are with you and do surround you with love and light. It is our desire that you open your hearts to receive that abundance that is already yours. Always we are with you. Our hearts are full and running over with love for each one.

You are each one, a prodigal son who has wandered far from home. Do you not remember all the Father has is yours also? When you do wake from your sleep and remember who you are, you will be welcomed by the outstretched arms of the Father and there will be the sound of great rejoicing, for the Father has waited long for your return. Man has wandered in the desert with only rare glimpses of what his true heritage might be. Now it is time to come home, home to the Father and that abundance of love, health, beauty and joy that has always been yours. Home to your rightful position as co-creator with the Father.

There is a great wave of light breaking over the earth like a brilliant sunrise and it is lighting the hearts and minds of those who open their hearts to receive. It is the sound of an angelic choir in one accord, thundering its majestic harmony across the planet as the light pours forth in all its brilliance.

All creation will truly awaken to who and what they are. The lion and the lamb will once again lie down together, for as the consciousness of man does change so does the consciousness of those creatures and all manifestation of life change. Not one entity upon the earth plane can make changes without supporting change in those manifestations about him. Is this not truly a wonderful thing?

This magnificent dawning of light upon the earth plane will be supported by the tender unconditional love of the Father. Each entity who wakens from his sleep will become aware of the opening of his heart center and the great swell of love that extends outward to all of those entities and those creatures upon the earth.

In this way all things will be healed, for love is that wonderful healing energy that opens the heart and the mind and frees one of those illusions that have kept mankind shrouded in a veil of fog, knowing there was another world, yet not able to see through the heavy mist. First love of oneself, then extending outward to all things and the inner knowing that all are one.

Encouragement

We are with you always, we are closer than your thoughts. We would guide you each of the days and the nights. You are never alone or without our love and protection. This is the way and the light for all of mankind but man knows it not. Since those days past when I descended into the earth plane, my energy has been with you, but many there are who have not awakened from their dream state and have not yet opened their awareness to me.

At this time, I draw near and strengthen the energy that I send forth, for it is the time of awakening. It is the time that all mankind is called upon to open their hearts and their minds and to receive me. I come in peace and I come in love. I come to lift them up and to bind their wounds, to hear their petitions and to answer all those whose hearts are open to receive. Each one upon the earth who opens their heart and who listens to that still small voice within does anchor my energy upon the earth. Each one who asks for guidance shall receive abundantly for I will hold nothing back.

This is the time of the "Second coming" which was long ago prophecized. It was said that "I come as a thief in the night," and thus it is. When there is even *one* whose heart is open, I steal quietly within. This time, dear ones, I do not come with fanfare or the sounding of trumpets, or a messenger before me. I enter silently those hearts that are open and I bring a message of love and light. Those of you on earth who receive my love, accept my message and who bring in the light of my body are the body of the Christ. Those will go forth in my name, not to preach the gospel, but to live the gospel and in so doing they embody my love and the light of my body upon the earth. For they are the word made manifest and they are my body made manifest in the material.

I bring through the hearts of many, the message of peace and the message of love. And those who will accept me go forth and love their neighbors even as they love themselves. As I am received into the hearts of man, even the least among you, I bring blessings to you and I fill you with light, for we are one, one, yet separate. This was the message of old, the promises of old, that the Father and Son are one and all that the Father has the son shall receive also, and so it shall be.

In those days past there were those things termed miracles and it was said, "What the Father does, you may do also, and even greater things than these." I say to you those prophecies of the past will come to be in the present. "Greater things than these you shall do." It shall be as it was said, many of you shall do greater things than has been done before. This is the time of the fulfillment of the law and the prophets, there is nothing to fear for I am with you always. I bring joy and healing to all those who would receive my love and power and my light. I am with you always. Those who receive my love and my spirit and carry it forth are truly my body manifest upon the earth. Not one who receives me shall go unnoticed.

As you go forth in peace, you shall be given the power for peace.

Peace will not come by the sword nor by force.

Peace will not come by the signing of treaties, though the signing of treaties may focus the awareness of some upon peace.

There have been many treaties signed in the history of this planet and yet there is war. Peace will come in the hearts of the many who will accept the Christ and the Christ Consciousness within and go forth to manifest peace in every part of his life. Peace with his family, but first, with self, then peace with his neighbor and peace within that country. I would say to you there are many who must make peace with their God for there are many who have fear and condemnation in their hearts for God, the Father. First they must make peace with self, then peace with God the Father.

There is not one among you who does not receive my love though there are many who turn their face away and are not aware of the light. Still I will be with these and I will offer my love again and again and again. Yet those who do not open their hearts to receive me and open their ears to hear me may need more time to come out of the heavy mist of fog into the light. They shall be given time, yet many of their brothers shall go on without them for not one shall stand still and as I have said, this is the time of awakening. This is the time when you are being called home, home to the Father!